Praise for *The Art of S*

"With clarity and authority, Dr. Thomson has written an essential guide for science communicators. This accessible and highly usable book can help readers better navigate the increasingly complex world of science communication."

—Barbara Natterson-Horowitz, MD
Faculty, Harvard Medical School – Harvard-MIT Health Sciences & Technology
Professor of Medicine, UCLA Division of Cardiology
President, International Society for Evolution, Medicine & Public Health
Best-selling author of *Zoobiquity* and *Wildhood*

"An engaging, practical manual in effective science communication. Dr. Thomson's passion for the collaborative elements of One Health shine throughout the book, yet her advice is equally applicable across all scientific disciplines. A great read for scientists and engineers at any point in their career- undergraduates, masters, PhD, post-doctorates and professionals, alike!"

—Simon Doherty, BVMS, CertAqV, CBiol, FRSB, FHEA, ARAgS, FRCVS
Past President, British Veterinary Association

"This book may not only help ensure the future of public health but the future of the planet by teaching people how to better understand and communicate on scientific topics. We need people like Dr. Deborah Thomson and her book, *The Art of Science Communication*, to inspire and teach us how to communicate about science in more clear, accurate, and engaging ways. No matter your profession, this book will take you on her personal journey from the classroom and exam room to working with policymakers in Washington, DC and give you specific advice and invaluable methods in the art of science communication."

—Teresa L. Schraeder, MD
Clinical Associate Professor
Director of the Communicator Scholarly Concentration
Warren Alpert Medical School, Brown University

"Effective communication is the bedrock of our social structures, and absolutely critical to successful advocacy. This book not only demystifies the policymaking process, it provides readers with fundamental communication techniques and strategies for engaging their audiences – whether private individuals or elected officials – and influencing positive outcomes."

—Kate Wall, JD
Senior Legislative Manager
International Fund for Animal Welfare

"A very accessible and effective book! It offers sound practical advice on science communication that you can start implementing right away to be more confident and convincing when talking about your work with children, friends, colleagues, and policymakers."

—Barbara Häsler, DVM, PhD
Senior Lecturer in Agrihealth
Royal Veterinary College
London, United Kingdom

"A must-read for scientists looking to communicate with policymakers! Dr. Thomson takes practical tips right out of the classroom for you to use."

—Andrea Stathopoulos, PhD
Professional Science Writer
2019–2021 AAAS Science and Technology Policy Fellow

"Dr. Deborah Thomson, DVM, is a wonderful educator and influential communicator. I highly recommend her writings for "single species" physicians and Public Health special staff officers. Dr. Thomson's guidance in policy development will empower subject matter experts from all disciplines. Cooperation, coordination, collaboration, and change, all depend on communication."

—William L Bograkos, MA, DO, FAOAAM, FACOFP, FACOEP, COL, MC, USA (retired)
Past President, American Osteopathic Academy of Addiction Medicine

"Dr. Thomson uses real life experiences and stories as a policy advisor, educator, and toastmaster to distill the stress of science communication into steps for success. Communicating at a classroom or at the Capitol, there's a little something for everyone."

—Edward van Opstal, PhD
Lead Scientist at Booz Allen Hamilton

"Engineers around the world will benefit from this book's information."

—David Beck, PhD Candidate
Systems Engineer, US Department of Defense

"If you're looking to improve how to effectively communicate with non-scientists and students of all ages, this is the book for you! Every chapter is full of real-world scenarios and offers practical techniques that any scientist, doctor, or professor can readily apply for immediate results."

—Nuno Carreiro, MS, DVM
Senior Lecturer, Department of Veterinary and Animal Sciences
University of Massachusetts-Amherst

"Dr. Thomson prepares the reader to be able to become a science advocate, engage with various audiences, receive research funding, and be comfortable discussing science no matter your specific background. These are all necessary skills for successful scientific communicators!"

—Simone B. Soso, PhD
Program Manager and Research Associate
Quality Education for Minorities Network

"Every scientist should be a science communicator. How Dr. Thomson successfully broke down the complex topic of One Health into simple and understandable lessons suitable for students as early as 6-year-olds is just brilliant. This book should be in the hands of all science schoolteachers and students. It has the potential to get more scientists, aspiring scientists, especially the next generation of women in STEM talking about science, joining science fields and advocating for better science."

—Doreen Onyinye Anene, PhD Researcher
The University of Nottingham, UK
Founder of The STEM Belle

"This book would definitely be useful for undergraduate and graduate students."

—Andrew Fang, PhD
2019–2021 AAAS Science and Technology Policy Fellow

"I wish this was required reading for every science and engineering student!"

—Madison Burns
Public Health Undergraduate Student
The George Washington University

"Having trouble communicating with clients at work? If so, this book was made for you!"

—Adam Christman, DVM, MBA
Chief Veterinary Officer, Fetch dvm360®

"The Art of Science Communication breaks barriers ..."

—Richard DiPilla
Founder, Global Goodwill Ambassadors Foundation

THE
ART OF SCIENCE
COMMUNICATION
Sharing Knowledge
with Students, the Public,
and Policymakers

DR. DEBORAH THOMSON

THE ART OF SCIENCE COMMUNICATION
Sharing Knowledge with Students, the Public, and Policymakers

© 2021 Thomson Publishing LLC

ISBN (paperback): 978-1-7371998-1-6

Cover art: Salvador Saenz
Cover design: MiblArt
Interior design: MiblArt
Editor: Sandra Wendel, Write On, Inc.

Published by Thomson Publishing LLC
Contact the author at www.Deborah-Thomson.com
LinkedIn: Deborah Thomson, DVM
Instagram: DeborahThomsonDVM
More information about One Health can be found at
www.OneHealthLessons.com

*To my parents, aunt, and brothers
who have been my unwavering supporters
from the beginning.
I am so lucky to have you in my life.*

CONTENTS

Prologue

The children were rambunctious my first day back in a classroom after a nine-year teaching hiatus. Their exasperated teacher greeted my friends and me with a polite smile and an apology; she explained her students were experiencing "cabin fever" since their recess time had to be spent indoors due to the local wildfires creating hazardous air outside.

Once the teacher had all thirty students seated at their desks and *almost* settled, she introduced the Science Guests—my three friends and me—a hodgepodge of adults: a water analyst, an insurance saleswoman, a sound engineer, and a veterinarian.

We were standing in front of thirty minimally focused eight- and nine-year-old children, to serve as science role models. Our mission was to make science fun, make it come to life, and make it both relatable and easy to understand. We were teaching a lesson I had designed about One Health, or the interconnection between our health and the health of the environment, animals, and plants.

Honestly, you could sit in a three-hour meeting that discusses the definition of One Health and still come out of it confused because the term is described as both a concept and an approach and is said to be abstract on both accounts. One Health is something that confounds many people but, with efficient communication techniques, anybody can understand it, and, even more importantly, start to care about it.

I opened the One Health lesson that day with a question: "Who here is a curious person?" I saw about three-quarters of the students raising their small hands. "What is she getting at?" I'm sure they were thinking. "Well, if you are curious," I declared, "then you will be a fantastic scientist!" A thoughtful look appeared on their faces.

I then introduced myself. "Hello, I'm Doctor Debbie, and I'm a veterinarian. Who can tell me what a veterinarian is?" I saw a hand dart up in the back left corner of the classroom.

The student confidently answered, "Somebody who only eats vegetables!"

I later realized this is not an uncommon answer from an eight-year-old. After all, veterinarian (or an animal doctor as I gently explained to the confused student) is a long word. Many adults have trouble saying it, let alone spelling it. Plus, a "vet" can also mean a military veteran. How confusing.

At the end of my first One Health lesson, I noticed a small dark-haired girl in a yellow blouse sitting near the back of the classroom. She was almost out of her seat, her raised arm extended before her, stretching her fingers in a way that looked like they were about to dislocate from her knuckles. She clearly had a burning question. She reminded me a lot of myself at that age.

I said "Okay, last question." The small child asked in an almost declaratory fashion, "Are you going to teach kids around the world about One Health?"

"Yes," I immediately replied. "But we need your help because we can't do it alone. How will you teach others in your family about One Health?"

That day, not only did we bring science to life, but we left the students with a call to action.

That is how the global One Health education movement was born. It started years ago in a single classroom in California near the wildfires. Since then, OneHealthLessons.com was launched, and the rest is a dream come true.

Within six months of publicly publishing my online COVID-19–focused One Health lessons for seven different age groups, hundreds of volunteers have been inspired to translate the lessons into over eighty languages. How is that possible? you may be asking. One word: inspiration. Volunteers from around the world learned of the importance of One Health; they saw the need to teach about it in their communities and in their own languages and wanted to bring the simple science lessons home.

Now, it is your turn to learn some practical science communication techniques, particularly those not typically found in a formal academic curriculum. These are tried-and-true techniques that I have discovered in various places—from the classroom, to the animal hospital, to public speaking competitions, and to one of the most powerful political offices in Washington, DC.

It is time for you to gain this knowledge and change the world.

1
Intention

From my experiences gained while teaching children about science, educating the general public about veterinary medicine, inspiring politicians to take action in support of and for the development of science-promoting policies, I have learned critical and practical lessons about science communication. My intention for this book is to provide guidance for you—the scientist—to successfully deliver your message and inspire action from your audience, whether it is to prevent people from littering in your neighborhood or convincing policymakers to increase funding for scientific research, particularly *your* research. With this book, it is no longer an excuse to say that there is insufficient science funding because it is up to us to convey the importance of our message to the right people at the right time.

Throughout this book, I use examples from my past and often utilize the idea of One Health as an example to drive home my message. This term can be quite contentious in certain circles as it has many long-winded definitions. For the sake of argument, for the remainder of the book, I am defining the concept of One Health as the interconnection between our health and the health of the environment, animals, and plants. Similarly, I am defining the One Health approach as teamwork between people of various strengths and backgrounds to prevent and efficiently solve complicated health problems (such as a pandemic).

For the COVID-19 pandemic, its resolution relies on the collaboration of professionals such as physicians, virologists, immunologists, veterinarians, social scientists, politicians, economists, educators, ecologists, engineers, health practitioners, and others. When I see such a list of stakeholders, I have many thoughts like: How many different scientific and professional languages would be spoken in these conversations? How often is there miscommunication? Are the participants satisfactorily conveying their message? How can everybody relate to and trust each other in order to efficiently solve this problem, especially when clear and practical communication skills have not been taught early in their professional training? In short, when you work together, you need to speak the same language.

I've seen the miscommunication problem firsthand. Years ago, when I was in my last few years of veterinary school, I tried to communicate complex medical conditions to pet owners who hadn't taken a science class in decades. It was incredibly challenging. A more recent example of miscommunication occurred when I was working in the largest Senate office on Capitol Hill and saw well-intentioned scientists inadvertently fail to deliver a meaningful message to the right policymakers at the right time. I know from experience that there is a steep learning curve for effective science communication and that old saying remains true: practice makes perfect.

This book is meant to inspire you to practice communication techniques in everyday life, and there is a strategic method to the layout of the book. I will first introduce you to communicating with people who are learning science for the first time (children); then I will move on to speaking with adults who likely forgot their primary and secondary school science because they no longer use it in their jobs. At the end, I will focus on speaking with influential adults, some who may surprise you, and who have the opportunity to change millions of lives with their decisions. How do you inspire *them* to believe in science?

It is now time to effectively communicate your own message to those outside your disciplinary bubble. If we want to practically solve major problems, we must (1) learn how to communicate science in a practical way and (2) practice the One Health approach. This book focuses on the first step.

2
What Is Science Communication?

Years ago, one person explained science communication to me as "a combination of facts, figures, and empathy." These three items are certainly important, but they are not the only ingredients used by influential science communicators.

Science communication allows us, the scientists (clinicians, engineers, social scientists, economists, bench researchers, and more), to speak with others outside of our professional bubble. Sometimes, facts and figures work in conveying our message. Other times, people only need to hear relatable stories. This book explains different practical communication techniques to use whenever you speak with people outside your immediate professional network.

Why is science communication important?

For centuries, the sciences have become so specialized that a physicist, for instance, is no longer a traditional physicist. Instead, she or he is either labeled a theoretical physicist or an applied physicist. The same occurrence is seen in the medical field: an interventional radiologist is not the go-to radiologist who would be only reading X-rays.

There are good and bad sides to this trend of specialization and ivision. The good side is that it permits more knowledge in niche fields and promotes scientific advancements. The bad side is that there are now disciplinary silos separating people. Unfortunately, these differences inhibit free communication and obstruct science wherever multidisciplinary research or work should be pursued.

When we apply for grant funding or even when we try to save a life in the hospital, we need to comfortably, persuasively, and efficiently communicate our thoughts and sense of urgency with others of different backgrounds and strengths. Through convincing another that your idea or project is the best to support, you are thereby meeting your needs. Like it or not, successful scientists know how to communicate outside of their bubble and convince others to support their cause.

Who can communicate science?

Any scientist, regardless of their discipline, would benefit from being an excellent communicator. When I describe the typical scientist to a child, I say that we are naturally curious people. We like to explore and push ourselves and expand our knowledge. We tend to work toward self-improvement. That is probably why you are reading this book.

With improved communication skills, you can
- Increase your chance of receiving grant money,
- Attract more people to volunteer as interns and graduate students in your lab,
- Act as a science role model to local children,
- Be viewed as an accessible expert in your field to journalists and others in the general public,
- Win more job interviews,
- Publish more articles, and
- For the medically inclined scientists, here is a special shout-out for you: efficiently translate medical terminolog⁻

into something understandable, which then allows you to treat your patient more efficiently.

Therefore, you can expand your career options in ways you could never have previously considered. It is time to keep reading.

When should science communication be taught?

In my opinion, science communication should be taught as soon as a student learns scientific language at the undergraduate level. In short, it is never too early to equip future scientists with life-long beneficial skills.

Why do some people not believe in science?

It is time to stop blaming others and start looking at ourselves. Look at all of medicine, and science, technology, engineering, and mathematics (STEM) as a whole, and consider if these disciplines are more exclusive, comprised of people who tend to not seek opportunities to communicate with others outside their bubble. Or are they inclusive?

It is not a person's fault if they don't believe in science. There is no time or need to judge them. There is only time to understand them and then determine and implement ways to communicate efficiently and effectively. As scientists of all disciplines, we must take the responsibility, as subject matter experts, to value the importance of being relatable. If we are not relatable then our message is less relatable. It is time to remember how life was before you knew your discipline so well. How foreign you must now sound to others outside your world. It is time for change. Let's get started.

3
How to Speak with Students about Science

Teaching children can change society—for better or for worse. Let's start with an example that can be disturbing to think about but happens in this world. Think of how many times you have heard about extremist groups focusing their energies on recruitment and indoctrination of children. Why do you think they do that? It is likely because they see the long-term benefit of ingraining an idea into society at the deepest level.

Some could argue that education is one of the most powerful weapons in the world because it can last multiple lifetimes. Now, let's imagine that a child becomes passionate about conservation at a young age. How would that affect her future? How would teaching millions of children about conservation change *the* future? Education gives me hope for a brighter future. We just need to do it right and ensure high-quality education is available to all. We can do that by serving as science role models and speaking about science with children.

Why scientists should speak with children

If you cannot explain your work to a child, you cannot explain your work effectively. There are multiple reasons why a scientist should speak to children about their work and professional interest. Not only does it create an environment where science seems more accessible to children, but you, the scientist guest in the classroom, serve as a relatable role model to students. It is likely that you would be valued as more than just a subject matter expert, particularly to that one child sitting in the back of the classroom who is hanging onto your every word. Instead, you represent the whole world of science. You are a scientist.

As a veterinarian visiting grade school classrooms to teach about One Health, I am mindful to explain to students that veterinarians (or animal doctors, as explained to the six-year-olds—and not vegetarians, as many children confuse the two) directly take care of every animal species other than people. However, by having a One Health mindset, veterinarians also help people indirectly by making sure that food like meat and eggs are safe to eat, to ensure that diseases shared between animals and people are kept at bay, by educating dog owners about vaccines for their pet, and more.

When this responsibility is explained to the students, their minds are opened about what a single profession can do. They see that veterinarians are not just playing with kittens and puppies all day (even though that would be extremely nice).

Every teacher who has welcomed me as a science guest in their classroom has expressed an interest in sharing new experiences with their students. It is okay to discuss science outside of your specific area if you are comfortable doing so. It is even okay to tell students that you don't know the answer. It is okay to encourage students to explore to find the answer themselves or, even better, search for it with a team.

Even if you are not going into classrooms as a guest speaker to teach a particular science lesson (like those found at OneHealthLessons.com), you may be asked to speak during a career day event. During those visits, like before, I recommend remaining open to speak about science as a whole. Like it or not, the students will likely see you as a "general scientist." Children are curious. They are like sponges. They ask questions—some that you can answer and others you cannot.

Sometimes they seem to ask random questions. For instance, after I taught a group of ten-year-olds about One Health, a student raised his hand and asked me how magnets worked. I smiled and could only go as far to explain positive and negative charges but, since the child did not understand the concept of atoms yet, I recommended he research the term *atom* with his parents at home (I then wrote the word on the board). That research would surely lead him down a rabbit hole. Who knows? Maybe he will become a particle physicist in twenty years.

As a final note here, if you are a university professor, think about how beneficial it would be to have your undergraduate, graduate, and doctoral students (particularly doctoral students) teach children. In general, the further removed a scientist is from their life prior to studies, the harder it is for them to communicate with people outside of their immediate scientific bubble. The mantra of "Learn It, Do It, Teach It" is ultimately the best way to ensure somebody thoroughly understands the topic.

The **take-home message** here is that speaking with children strengthens your communication skills, regardless of your ultimate target audience, because children show you exactly how they feel. Later in the book, we will review techniques to use when speaking with policymakers and their staff, which may feel like communicating through an opaque theater curtain. Take this time to hone your ills by speaking with children so that your communication talents shine when the spotlight is really on you.

How scientists should speak with children

Whenever I start teaching a lesson about One Health to children, I always open with a question: "Who here is a curious person? Raise your hand if you are curious." After seeing some hands raised, I then say, "If you are a curious person, then you will be an excellent scientist!"

By speaking directly to children, STEM career folks become more accessible and more relatable. It creates a perception that your STEM discipline is also obtainable to those students. Instead of teaching children in a lab coat, I teach in my regular street clothes—be it a hoodie or a T-shirt. I do this on purpose. I do this to make science more accessible and relatable. After the students get accustomed to seeing me in everyday clothes, sometimes I put on my stethoscope so that I could appear to transform before their eyes. That way, they see me as a single person with two identities: both as a private individual and as a veterinarian serving my community.

When speaking to children about your professional discipline, the best way to capture a child's attention is by getting them to laugh and play. After teaching your class, a friendly classroom trivia competition is always a hit for secondary school students. The students can win bragging rights (which are free and calorie-free as well). For younger students, in primary school, time dedicated to drawing what they learned in picture form is another excellent way to summarize lessons learned during the day.

Scientists educate families by teaching children

For years, I have created lessons about One Health for children and have taught them in primary and secondary schools. The experience has taught me that children who were excited ab what they learned in class can then go home and educate their own families.

Don't believe me? I received an email from a nine-year-old after a One Health lesson was taught to his class. During that One Health lesson, the students learned about antigenic shift (which happens with influenza causing swine flu as well as other viruses). His email went like this:

> Dear Scientist Guests,
> I learned that when two viruses come inside one body of an animal, it [can make] a new one. That was ... my favorite part! When I told my family that, they were surprised ... Also, my second favorite part [of] the [s]cience [class] was when [we combined] two sentences together and [they created] a new [mutated sentence]. I hope that you'll come again during our Science [class] ...

From my experience, the best technique to inspire children's interest in science (where they explain the lesson to their parents) is to get them to laugh, play, and investigate solutions to a problem. During the lesson, encourage students to ask questions. Support their curious nature. Act as a scientist role model and get them to forget that they are learning while focusing on the activity or game presented to them. Once you get young students laughing, just like with adults, your audience is more likely to remember the lesson and underlying message.

Think of children as stem cells

Do you want to change policy that affects the future? Do you also want to change future policy development? One way to do this is to speak with children.

As you read in the previous section, children can educate older generations in their own families. Imagine if a child was teaching their parent (who is conveniently an elected official) about climate change. Imagine that this child can explain that analyzing the ratio between Carbon-13 and Carbon-14 proves that the bulk of carbon dioxide in the Earth's atmosphere comes from man-made sources. Imagine that a quiet child is sitting in the back of your classroom and is intently listening to you during your science guest appearance. She is silently processing the information, and there is a real chance that your words could influence her daily choices as well as her future career trajectory.

A child is like a stem cell that can develop in many different ways. Children may become parents and grandparents and educate their offspring. Children may become teachers and educate their future students. Children may become scientists, politicians, technicians, engineers, clinicians, mathematicians, and more. Education is so powerful it can affect generations. Living and learning go hand in hand.

How communicating with children will benefit you

With so many years of study after secondary school, you may not remember the vocabulary you once used. You even may forget what you knew and didn't know at what age. It may be difficult to communicate your professional thoughts and breakthroughs with people outside of your career circle. Does this sound like you? Could this limit you? Can you easily explain to your neighbor what the title of your PhD thesis actually means in relation to everyday life for the average person?

I remember attending a graduation ceremony at a prestigious university, and I could not understand two-thirds of the graduate thesis titles listed in the program. There was so much discipline-specific terminology. To think if this type of arcane terminology is used in the title and text of a project (which should be accessible and understandable to everyone), I can only imagine how difficult it would be to convey the message of the research in order to influence politicians toward policy adoption and grant money distributions. I would imagine it would be next to impossible to convey this message—that is, if they did not read this book.

Some of the best ways to communicate your thoughts in a clear and concise manner are to speak with children who tend to have short attention spans and to participate in regular Toastmasters International meetings (details about Toastmasters is coming up). The more time you spend speaking in classrooms and with the general public and policymakers, your comfort level and confidence will significantly increase.

4
How to Speak with the Public about Science

efore you read further, put this book down, go to www.
toastmasters.org/find-a-club and sign up to be a guest at a local Toastmasters International meeting. After that, please read on.

What I learned from Toastmasters

Toastmasters International is a public speaking organization that has taught me a lot. It has taught me how to tailor a story to meet the needs of my audience. It has taught me how to actively listen and how to provide feedback in a manner that is helpful to the speaker but also provides constructive guidance. It has taught me how to think on my feet with its mandatory impromptu speaking activity known as Table Topics. During this intimidating portion of the meeting, a club member is asked an unexpected question and has up to two minutes to answer it without using crutch words such as *um, so, you know, ah, look* (you get the point).

Learning the technique of effective communication takes practice. Toastmasters exists for you to practice. I am certain that practicing impromptu speaking over the last six years with weekly

Toastmasters meetings has created new career opportunities for me. When transitioning from practicing clinical veterinary medicine in the animal hospital to serving as a science policy advisor in the office of a polished and respectable politician in the United States Senate, I experienced an hour-long interview with random questions flying at me from all directions. Even though I practiced every night in the month leading up to the interview, I was only asked one question that I predicted. Everything else was unexpected. Thank goodness I could think on my feet! Thank goodness for Toastmasters! Look for local chapters of Toastmasters in your area. If you don't have one, then start one.

I joined Toastmasters because, despite having teaching experience, I had difficulty explaining medicine to my patient's (the animal's) owners. I wanted to speak effectively on behalf of my silent patients so the owners could make the best decisions for their animal.

After being surrounded by veterinary and medical students during the years dedicated to attaining my veterinary degree, I only spoke one language—that of medicine. I used words like *elimination* and *excrement* instead of *pee* and *poo*. I used adjectives like *fractured* instead of *broken* or *chipped*. I was not used to speaking Plain English anymore. I recognized I must immediately surround myself with people who were not familiar with medicine. I had to re-immerse myself into society. Fortunately, I found a large Toastmasters club in 2014 and never looked back. Long story short: if you want to make your science understandable, join Toastmasters.

"If you don't remember anything else, remember this."

Every time you speak to an audience, whittle your message down to a single sentence. If you are giving a talk with a visual slide show, be sure to have one slide entitled "Take-Home Message." Make sure you say this message at least twice during your talk. During the last time you state the sentence, preface it with, "If you don't remember anything else, remember this," and then say the sentence.

This phrasing helps break up the pacing of your presentation. It also brings the audience's attention back to the words you are using and reinforces your overall message.

Tell a story

I once heard somebody say that telling a science story humanizes science. I like that. Telling a story at the start of your talk with members of the general public is a strategic way to deliver a message.

Don't have a story that is relatable to your particular background? Then explain to the audience why you decided to go into your field of choice. I often share the story of when I realized I wanted to be a veterinarian. Unlike many of my classmates in veterinary school, who seemed to have known since they left their mother's womb, I didn't know I wanted to be a vet until I was twenty-one.

As a naturally curious person, I considered being an architect, a musician, a statistician, a physician, a teacher, an ecologist, and more. But nothing was really grabbing my attention. Sure, I thought these topics were interesting, but nothing stopped me in my tracks. Like love at first sight. It wasn't until I started shadowing some veterinarians when I realized that, with my single actions, I could help animals *and* the people relying on those animals for food, for milk, and for companionship.

I remember I was taking a marine biology course and was sitting on a finely grained white sand beach, my sun-kissed feet were partially buried in the cool sand, and I was sitting halfway under a slightly swaying palm tree, with crystal-clear light turquoise water before me. I looked to my right, down the secluded beach, and thought to myself, I'd rather be in a veterinary hospital right now. If that wasn't an "Aha!" moment, I don't know what is.

By making yourself more relatable and painting a picture, you indirectly make your scientific message more relatable. People are not born as educated scientists, but people are naturally curious. After all, isn't this characteristic what originally led you to science?

Build your message

A story can help build your message as long as it is not seen as a tangent. First decide what you want your audience to feel and do once your presentation ends, and then start crafting your message.

If there is an "Aha!" moment in your story, make that single meaningful point neatly reflect your take-home message. As it is sometimes difficult to deliver a story with a true "Aha!" moment, you may elect to choose a longer story line. If this is the case, ensure that your relatable story ties into your overall message at the beginning, middle, and end. Frequently reflect to that initial story throughout the remainder of your talk while you are adding layers to your message.

While building your message, keep it as simple as possible. Work toward a single goal. Remember to answer these questions while crafting your story:

- What do you want your audience to remember from your time together?

- Do you want them to share your story or your overall message? If yes, how? If no, why not?
- What action do you want them to take, if any?

Speaking with the public about a controversial topic

There are three rules to remember when speaking with the public about a controversial topic: be honest, education is power, and lead the conversation.

Rule 1: Be honest.

Science is always changing with new discoveries. Sometimes, science reverts backward because a recent discovery disproves a past and generally accepted theory. The general public does not understand that this is the way science works.

Take medicine for example. Clinicians (such as physicians, veterinarians, and dentists) read many journals discussing new therapeutics, new standards of care, and new discoveries and then translate this hard science into something applicable to their patients. Clinicians, just like researchers, are only human. However, a person sick in a hospital does not want to think of their physician as a human who is capable of making a mistake. Patients trust physicians with their lives. There is a lot at stake in making a mistake.

Sometimes, however, a clinician does not know why the patient (person or animal) is sick. Sometimes it is due to ignorance or inexperience of the clinician, but other times it is due to the fact that this is a new disease. The clinician might wonder, Did the pathogen just mutate from the local animal population or is it an atypical presentation of a known disease?

Was it transmitted to the person by a new tick in the area? Did the person drink water contaminated by an unknown toxin, possibly a by-product of another chemical previously deemed harmless in the environment?

When clinicians do not know the answer to why somebody is sick, it is okay to say, "I don't know," but be sure to follow this up with, "But I will consult with a colleague or specialist to give you the best possible chance of feeling better."

Rule 2: Education is power.

A controversial topic such as climate change is only controversial because of the lack of niche knowledge and trust. The lack of knowledge is not stupidity. Remember, everybody must be treated with respect and be understood in order to deliver science in the most meaningful way.

I have spoken with people who do not believe in climate change. Some of these people work in the US Federal Government. In particular, these people recognize that the planet is changing but do not believe the changing climate is due to human involvement. I am not surprised by this belief. After all, it is much less stressful to believe the changes occurring to our planet were inevitable and have nothing to do with people's actions. Guilt is an uncomfortable emotion that people tend to avoid.

Now, how could we change the minds of climate change deniers? Can we start talking about Carbon-13 and Carbon-14? Remember, the general public does not commonly understand isotopes. Their last chemistry class was probably back in secondary school, and, even then, they didn't like the subject very much. However, the general public does know about carbon dioxide and that more carbon dioxide in the atmosphere is problematic because it warms the planet. They may know this because it has been repeated over and over again on television and in the news. They may not understand it, but they tend to accept it as fact due to repetition.

What the general public doesn't recognize is *the reason* why scientists say climate change is being exacerbated by human activity. The public typically does not know that scientists can determine the original source of the carbon that is in the carbon dioxide molecules floating up in the atmosphere. However, they do know that we inhale oxygen and exhale carbon dioxide.

Therefore, it is not necessary to explain to the public exactly what isotopes are. The important point is to explain that there are different versions of carbon and those versions come with their own assigned numbers. Through years of research, scientists know that Carbon-13 comes from fossil fuels and Carbon-14 comes from living plants. When sampling carbon dioxide in the atmosphere, we have discovered there is a large percentage of Carbon-13 up there. Therefore, fossil fuels are worsening the thickening atmosphere.

Once the general public understands that, they may start to make more eco-friendly decisions. Remember, trust in science is never guaranteed. We, as scientists, need to work to make the scientific process and its discoveries as accessible as possible. We do that by using our communication skills.

Rule 3: Lead a conversation.

Once you explain a concept like climate change with a public audience, then you should welcome a conversation. Encourage them to ask questions. Show empathy while they ask these questions. Understand that their questions will often come from a place of unfamiliarity with the subject and not from malice. Everybody is entitled to respect. Show that you are actively listening and try to determine the reasons behind their comments.

I often say phrases like, "I can see why people think that. I once thought that too, but this is what I was taught since." Notice how I said how I was taught instead of saying I learned. By saying you were taught, others see you as more relatable because you were once a student.

After recognizing their thoughts and comments, you can then describe up to two scientific climate-related discoveries that support your (scientifically sound) statements, but avoid overwhelming your audience with facts. (Remember, you can have too much of a good thing.) If you are patient enough, you will see the crowd shift in your favor as long as they feel recognized and understood.

This is an occasion for you, the scientist, to listen and learn as much as your audience. Each conversation is a learning opportunity to improve your own science communication skills.

Talk to journalists

A wise man, who is constantly being interviewed, privately told me that once you are seen as an expert in a field by one journalist, word travels fast among other journalists. In addition, as will be discussed in the policymakers chapter, you may be invited to speak with influential offices that may craft policy and laws after you are noticed in a high-profile article. The potential of spreading your message is substantial if you secure at least one journalist fan.

However, a word to the wise: keep your message clear and simple and use a positive tone. For instance, avoid saying something like, "People erroneously think that climate change is a hoax and scientists are foolish," because that sentence can be easily edited to a new sound bite of "climate change is a hoax and scientists are foolish," which you did actually say. Instead, say something like, "Human-made climate change does exist, and we know that because scientists have measured different carbon types in the atmosphere and can trace the source of the carbon back to the usage of fossil fuels like oil or coal."

Four steps to change the minds of others

From my personal experiences in the classroom, at the animal hospital, and in a congressional office, I will describe an effective way to not only change people's minds but also inspire them to accept the change.

Step 1: Respect comfort zones.

It may sound counterintuitive, but the first step to changing the minds of people is to talk about the inherent benefits of *not* changing. Recognize that not changing will be much simpler, and people generally take comfort in the status quo. Plus, not changing requires a lot less from people—less energy, less worry, less potential struggle.

Let's use an example of speaking with a vaccine-hesitant person. During your conversation with this person, listen to why they distrust the science that legitimizes vaccine development and administration. In 2021, despite people being affected by the COVID-19 pandemic for over twelve months, a substantial portion of the American population has refused the COVID-19 vaccine. Instead of becoming angry and/or frustrated, scientists need to be empathetic and listen. Once a person feels heard by another, there is more opportunity to build trust in the relationship. Therefore, the first step is to actively listen and see the world from their perspective.

Step 2: Talk about the costs of changing one's mind.

This also may sound counterintuitive. Why would you want to voice concerns about the cost(s) of change? (Costs can include a person's energy investment of moving outside of their comfort zone and being open to both unlearning and then learning new information.) The simple answer, that you may not want to hear, is that your audience is thinking about this cost anyway, so you may as well get the topic out in the open. This also demonstrates that you share the same thoughts as your listener. Building upon the first step, this move provides you an added layer of intimacy and makes you appear more relatable.

Taking the vaccine-hesitant conversation one step further, the cost of changing would equate to having the vaccine-hesitant person actually receive the COVID-19 vaccine. It is worth voicing that the vaccine was created in record time, which is both impressive and mystifying to many. Even though the basic science behind the creation of the mRNA vaccine has been around for decades (for more information, search online for Katalin Karikó), there wasn't enough funding to complete the development of mRNA vaccines until the COVID-19 pandemic flipped the world upside down.

The cost of changing (or, in this case, of getting the COVID-19 vaccine) would address the fact that it is possible to have one or more vaccine reactions such as feeling ill for a few days to a few weeks, contingent on a person's immune system.

Depending on what type of vaccines are available, there is a chance a booster is needed. This booster further challenges the immune system and improve its strength to fight the actual virus that causes COVID-19 (SARS-CoV-2). The timing of the booster vaccine is of vital importance as well. If the person (or animal) receiving vaccines is not receiving the booster in a time period that is deemed acceptable for that particular vaccine, they may need to restart the series because of the way the immune system functions. This point bears repeating: the need to restart the vaccine series is not the fault of the vaccine; instead, it is due to the nature of the immune system. The importance of timing of vaccines and their boosters should be discussed so that nobody feels a false sense of security and takes unnecessary risks to their own health. In addition, it is important to review that vaccines are designed to strengthen the immune system but the person (or animal receiving the vaccine) could still technically become infected and sick by the pathogen. They just likely won't die from the disease. Again, vaccine side effects can happen and are worth acknowledging. Transparency is key.

Step 3: Address the costs of not changing.

Once empathy and trust are established, advance to this step. The goal is to cajole the listener to say "that's right" at least once. Focus on the possible lost opportunities with inaction during this step.

Furthering the COVID-19 vaccine conversation, review how the world changed from 2019 to 2020. Share a story about one or several missed opportunities. Talk about what your expected future would be if not enough people got vaccinated. Would much change for the overwhelmed hospitals and, particularly, the first responders and essential workers found in them? (Tip: Emphasizing people rather than systems or buildings strengthens the message.)

Review that vaccinated people could likely still catch a virus, but they would be less likely to die from the virus. Ask what the vaccine-hesitant person thinks of this idea. Talk about why you had decided to wear your mask and socially distance yourself from others outside your home for many months. Ask them why they took (or didn't take) certain actions during the pandemic. Talk about why you are tired of being afraid of a deadly virus and staying away from loved ones in order to protect them. Ask the hesitant person how they are feeling. Talk about the only way you can stop being afraid is if more people get vaccinated. Talk about how you are tired of seeing sad news reports of the total daily COVID-19 death count. Ask them how we all can get through this together.

(At the time of writing this book, health experts say that the answer is to continue wearing face masks that cover a person's nose and mouth, keep good personal hygiene habits, and vaccinate more people.) Once you hear the vaccine-hesitant person say "that's right" at least once, you can move on to the final step.

Step 4: End on a high note.

This step brings hope. This is when you speak about the benefits of change. By now, the listener is in agreement with you. It is time to talk about the future in a positive light.

For the COVID-19 conversation, this is where you would ideally hear the other person volunteer to say that they will get the vaccine. However, the world is far from ideal.

Therefore, it is your job to end the conversation on a high note. Say that you live in less fear since you have been vaccinated because you know that you have strengthened your immune system in case you encountered the deadly virus. You can now see your fully vaccinated family and friends with less worry. You can now start to imagine your future beyond the pandemic, thanks to your strengthened immune system, which ultimately resulted from your decision to receive your vaccine(s).

5
How to Speak with Staff
of Policymakers about Science

U nless you are at the top of a global industry like Bill
Gates, chances are high that you will not meet the elected
official on your first visit. Instead, you need to convince the
politician's staff (referred to as "staffers" by insiders on Capitol
Hill in Washington, DC) to be on your side and then accurately
deliver your message to the elected official.

As a science policy advisor in the largest (non-committee)
office in the United States Senate, I have sat on the "other side"
of the boardroom table and listened to pitches from numerous
well-intentioned scientists. Sometimes after meeting with the
scientific visitors, my policy colleagues would irately say, "Did
they *really* just explain what a [fill in the blank with something
obvious] was to me?" At other times, after a meeting with
scientists, my colleagues would ask me, "Can you please write
up notes from that meeting and say it in a way that can be
understood?" or even "They never asked us for anything, why
did they schedule the meeting?"

It is clear that the well-intentioned scientist, engineer,
physician, veterinarian, environmental scientist, sociologist,
animal welfare advocate, or whoever else was requesting the

meeting missed the mark. If you see yourself wanting to share your message with any politician's office, this chapter will be helpful.

Feel free to highlight, circle words, scribble notes, and discuss this chapter with colleagues before approaching any lawmaker's office. This chapter will lift the opaque curtain and give you an insider's insight based on my experience on Capitol Hill in Washington, DC. While this section of the book is based on my experience working with the US Federal Government, you could apply these tips at the local and state levels. Similarly, for scientists outside the United States, please read this section with an open mind and explore how you can apply this advice to leaders in your own community, your own district, and your own country.

Understand Capitol Hill (specific to the United States)

In the United States, the House of Representatives (called the House) has smaller offices than those associated with the Senate. That is important to know for a few reasons:

The House staff are stretched much thinner than Senate staff. For instance, one staff member can be in charge of developing policy in science, space, agriculture, housing, and education for their boss in the House while, in the Senate, each of these topics would typically be covered by one or two people. Generalizing, that means that the Senate staff has more in-depth knowledge on certain areas of policy. This is by no means a hard-and-fast rule.

Early in my experience on the Hill, I realized that there are brilliant people working in offices in both the House of Representatives and the Senate, and from all political persuasions, so it is safe to assume that when you are taking a meeting with any staff, they know their stuff.

Second, the House staff are highly focused on their individual districts; whereas, the Senate staff think of the state as a whole. Certainly, this is another generalization but something that is confused by visitors. One representative in the House represents several hundreds of thousands of people, and one senator may represent several million. Therefore, when approaching a senator's office with a policy idea, make sure to include why this policy is important for people in that state. (You win more points if you relate your topic to a wide range of people and areas within the state.) Similarly, drive home the point about the effects of a policy in the home district of a representative.

All too often I'd hear a respectable bill idea but see it as an opportunity for another office to lead because it would not directly affect the constituents (or voters) of the Senator's state.

Take-home message: do not waste your time speaking with the wrong office.

Similar to knowing the priority of the congressperson, be certain you know what congressional committees the elected official sits on because science policy bills are reviewed by committees (prior to being voted on by the entire Senate or House of Representatives). It is especially important to know if the official is the Chair or the Ranking Member of that committee. These two positions have the most power in the committee and often determine what policy bill is reviewed and what is ignored.

A Committee Chair is the person who is the leader of a congressional committee and who is a member of "the majority" or more powerful political party (either Democrats, Republicans, or Independents). The only way one political party is more powerful than the other is if it holds the majority of seats. For instance, in the United States Senate, there are 100 seats filled by 100 elected senators (two from each state). Therefore, any political party with at least fifty elected senators (along with the potentially tie-breaking Vice President who is affiliated with the same party) is the most powerful.

This is why it is so important for people to vote every two years, and not every four years. The checks and balances inherent in the US Constitution depend on everybody's vote. Voting every two years is even more important for the House of Representatives because all representatives can lose their seat or position every two years. This is in comparison to the Senate where one-third (approximately thirty-three seats) are up for reelection every two years. This one-third could be enough to flip the Senate, giving substantial power to a different political party. **Take-home message:** vote in every election offered in your area.

For your awareness, a Committee's Ranking Member is the most influential person coming from the minority party (the political party with fewer than half seats filled) in the committee. Even though the Chair is more powerful than the Ranking Member, there is often a lot of communication between those two officials.

Again, choose the right office to visit.

Understand the role of the district offices

There is substantial influence on the elected official coming from the district office(s) because these offices have their finger on the pulse of the community. If you meet with staff in the home state, then be sure to relate your message to the local community in an obvious way. Also, try to attend and speak up at town hall meetings where the congressmember would be present. It is smart to bring a one-pager (be aware that some call this a "position paper") about your science policy idea to the meeting (see an example in Appendix C).

Understand the hierarchy within a personal (not committee) office

I had the unique opportunity to work in the largest office in the United States Congress as the only (to my knowledge) science-trained policy advisor. However, that was not my title even though that was my role. My first official title was Legislative Fellow, and then I was hired on to be a full-time employee as a Legislative Assistant.

There are many different roles in an elected official's office on Capitol Hill in Washington, DC. And, as you have previously read, one staff member can be responsible for different policy areas within their "portfolio" (or topics they are responsible for). Some offices work differently, but I will give you an overall layout of the congressional office hierarchy. In short, here is the general hierarchy of personal (not committee) offices on Capitol Hill.

- **Intern:** This person is not a full-time congressional staff member but assists in the daily running of the office. This person is typically an undergraduate student or recent graduate and is in the office for a few months.
- **Staff Assistant:** This full-time staff member typically answers the phones and welcomes you in the office.
- **Legislative Correspondent** ("LC"): This full-time staff member writes the first draft of letters for the elected official to voters and works closely with a Legislative

Assistant to address topics in the Legislative Assistant's portfolio.

- **Legislative Assistant** ("LA"): This full-time staff member directly serves the elected official. Often, she or he creates policy ideas and action items for the elected official to consider. In addition, this person meets with constituents and lobbyists, crafts letters on behalf of their boss to other federal or state officials and government agencies, and creates legislation (like bills) and then works behind the scenes to inspire other staffers (of other offices) to bring the bill to the attention of their own boss. (As you can imagine, this behind-the-scenes effort works best when the elected official also directly requests their peers to support the legislation.)
- **Legislative Director** ("LD"): This full-time staff member manages all the aforementioned people. This person has constant contact with the elected official and generally meets weekly with other Legislative Directors (of their political party) on the Hill to get a general sense of the political climate.
- **Chief of Staff:** This full-time staff member is essentially managing the entire office and keeps the elected official up-to-date on everything that she or he needs to know.
- **The elected official:** This person is the boss. The Senator or the Representative (often referred by Hill folks as the Congresswoman, the Congressman, or Congressperson). Whatever she or he says, goes. Depending on the type of person and leadership style, this person relies on the quality of their staff to varying degrees and on various subjects. This person has the final word. The consequences of their actions can be massive, and there is always a risk that this official will not be reelected.

Please keep in mind that the position of a Hill staffer can be transient due to elections every two years in the House of Representatives and every six years in the Senate. In addition, it is common to see staff turnover within a two- to three-year span, particularly in less-experienced Hill offices.

Auxiliary Staff (or aides not found in every personal office) are these:

Research Assistant: This person is devoted to help research material in preparation for legislative action (bill creation, letters to other officials, assist Legislative Correspondents and Legislative Assistants, and more).

Legislative Fellow: There are several sources of Fellows on Capitol Hill. I was associated with both the American Association for the Advancement of Science (who trained me) and the American Veterinary Medical Association (who paid my annual stipend). For the record, I was not a lobbyist nor had any interaction with the American Veterinary Medical Association other than contacting them for technical assistance during my Fellowship position (you will learn more about technical assistance later on).

Other Fellows can be affiliated with the other professional societies, Brookings Institute, ORISE (Oak Ridge Institute for Science and Education), the military, and some federal agencies. It is best to assume that if you are speaking with a Fellow, they have won a competitive application process to achieve their current position, and they provide free assistance as a full-time but temporary subject-matter expert to their congressional office. They may have more flexibility with their portfolio, depending on the office. It is worth asking about the breadth of the policy areas they manage so that you get a better sense of whom you are speaking with.

Counsel: This person is an attorney who (depending on the office) is either at the same level as a Legislative Assistant or higher than a Legislative Assistant.

Deputy Chief of Staff: This person is the office manager directly reporting to the Chief of Staff and is placed above the Legislative Director.

In general, if you are unsure with whom you are speaking (and where they place in this hierarchy), then look at their business card at the start of the meeting. The title is directly under their name, which is directly under the raised golden eagle emblem.

Age is just a number

Do not be surprised if you see a twenty-year-old greet you when you arrive at a congressional office. Similarly, the staff you will meet in the boardroom will likely also have a youthful appearance. Capitol Hill tends to be swarming with twenty- and thirty-something staffers who ... know their stuff. Trust them. They would not have been hired if they didn't know their stuff.

Government funding and deadlines

It may sound surprising, particularly after watching the news, but Congress actually has deadlines. One such deadline that is important for you to know about is focused on the time when Congress makes a decision to give a certain amount of taxpayer money to something like a federal agency (this is called Appropriations).

This is **what you need to know:** reach out to your US Representative in late January or early to mid-February with ideas and requests of how much money should go where.

Before approaching them, find answers to the following questions: What type of research funding is important to you? For instance, should money go toward the National Institutes of Health so that they can then spend this money to support various grants across the country? When approaching Senate offices with requests for Appropriations, this can be done in February, March, or very early April. As you can see, the House tends to finalize their funding decisions earlier than the Senate.

Every office has its own deadline. You need to determine what deadline is important to you based on your home state and district. Don't know what is involved in "reaching out" to your one US Representative and two US Senator offices? Find the office phone numbers online and call them. Be sure to say that you are a constituent (a voter represented by the elected official).

Ask the office if there are "appropriation request forms" that should be completed before taking a meeting with a staff member. The meeting would be a way to further explain why you feel money should be given to help a particular mission. There are more details about taking meetings with congressional staff later in this chapter. But before covering that, there are a few other items to mention.

Understand the staff member you are speaking with

Regardless if you are speaking with a Legislative Correspondent or someone higher in the hierarchy, they all have direct access to the Congressional Research Service for confidential consultations with subject matter experts. These experts often have post-doctorates or other professional degrees in their field. They know their stuff. It is best to assume that the person you are speaking with knows more than the general public, but don't expect them to know niche-specific jargon. And avoid acronyms at all costs while speaking with staff (unless they start doing it themselves)!

Understand the political climate

One of my favorite phrases while working on the Hill was, "A good idea at the wrong time is not a good idea." Remember that. Highlight it. Write it on your mirror. Use it as a screen saver on your computer or phone. *Timing. Is. Everything.*

Read the public reports coming out of that official's website within the week before your meeting with the office. Is there any news about the official in the newspaper? Any recent interview? Any scandal? What is on the official's mind?

I remember somebody approached the office to discuss an idea for 2021 during the onset of the COVID-19 pandemic (January/February of 2020). That was the wrong move. Another example of poor timing is when there was a natural disaster occurring that morning in the Senator's state and somebody came into the office and attempted to joke around at the start of the meeting. Bad move. Those were poor decisions on both of their parts. Do not be that person. Look around you and read the room.

Understand the priorities of the elected official

This reflects what is mentioned in the next chapter on how to speak with policymakers about science. As a preview, know the official's long-standing voting record on the subject of interest. Find out if she or he has been supportive of your mission. If the politician has not been supportive, try to use your time with the staff to understand the reason why.

Approach this delicate conversation in a neutral way and show that you are genuinely curious. If you show signs of aggression or being defensive or offensive while asking the question, you will not get the truth. In the end, you may not get a direct answer, but it is worth trying to understand the reason for the vote history because that is the first step to change the official's and staffers' minds. You can then arrange a follow-up meeting in one month to continue the conversation.

Create a one-pager

All too often, as a staff member in the United States Senate, I received a package of papers during a meeting with scientists to "look through at my own convenience." I would say, on average, after looking at the papers in the packet over thirty seconds, the most helpful piece of information is the one-pager. This is like currency on the Hill. Please note that I did not say a two-page document. I said a one-page document. Two pages is one page too long, as I once learned during the congressional orientation session with the American Association for the Advancement of Science (AAAS).

This single page has the science policy's objective, how it affects the state's constituents, how it looks good, how it can look bad (politicians need to know both sides of a policy idea before making a decision), who already supports the policy idea, and how much the policy change would cost the country. Don't just note the problem. List at least three realistic solutions! Remember that every policy idea revolves around feasibility, timing, and money.

Are you a voter in the official's district?

If so, wonderful. Make sure to clearly state that fact near the beginning of the meeting. If not, you need to have somebody else with you to serve that role. Some offices do not allow meetings with the staffers if there is no constituent (voter) present. In the offices that accept meetings without any current constituents present, in general, your message will not be as impactful.

Come with an "ask"

If you don't make the reason for your visit clear in the first quarter of the meeting, then you are wasting your time and the staffers' time. Staffers do not generally like meet-and-greet meetings where the only purpose is an introduction. Their time, like yours, is precious. They work in twenty-minute or less increments. Their deadlines are strict, and consequences of missing the deadline can have national ramifications. Information needs to be exchanged during the meeting.

To prepare for your meeting, ask yourself these questions:
- What is the problem that needs to be addressed and what are several feasible (meaning cost-effective and likely bipartisan) solutions to the problem?
- What should the staff consider during and after your meeting together?
- Have you stated the key points that you included in your one-pager (for an example, see Appendix C)? (Remember, there is a chance the staff doesn't even look at the one-pager so your verbal message should reinforce what is said in print.)

Pronounce the elected official's name correctly

On average, I heard visitors mispronounce my boss's name about 35 percent of the time. This easily correctable blunder loses the visitor's credibility at the exact moment the mispronounced name passes their lips. If you are taking the time to come in to share your idea or mission, then take the time to listen to an online interview with the politician. I'm certain their name will be said. Play it on repeat until you can correctly say the politician's name effortlessly.

Know your allies

If you know that a well-respected nonprofit or think tank supports the message you are delivering to the office, then say so. If you know that this group has publicly supported legislation that the elected official has created, then it is definitely worth mentioning the group by name. To determine which groups have supported this politician's actions that align with your scientific mission, do some online research. Are there any editorials published? Search by keywords. Once you have identified your allies and know that they are in good standing with the politician, then you may consider saying something like, "[Nonprofit name] that supported your boss's legislation on [subject] says on their website that [something you are trying to emphasize] is the best way to approach the topic we are discussing." Make sure that this point is also included in your one-pager with a hyperlink to the aforementioned website.

If you are stumped and cannot find any other allies prior to the meeting with the staff, then it wouldn't hurt to ask the staff at the end of your meeting who else has approached them to discuss this topic. Any nongovernment organizations? Any think tanks? Any universities? From there, you can try to synergize your efforts during their regularly scheduled annual or biannual "lobby day" (if your potential allies have one, which they likely do).

Show appreciation

Chances are, you had your hopes up to engage with the elected official. Don't be disheartened if you speak only with the staff. Ultimately, you want the staff on your side because they are the ones who are always around the elected official.

It is safe to assume that staff are incredibly busy and are getting pulled in many different directions. To make the best first impression, follow these steps:

1. Arrive five minutes before your meeting.
2. Do not go over time. Typically, meetings are twenty minutes. You are lucky if you get thirty. If you are not sure of the expected duration, then ask at the beginning and express that you want to be respectful of their time.
3. Have your business cards ready to exchange at the start of the in-person meeting.
4. Do make eye contact and show that you are actively listening.
5. Do have an "ask" and make it clear in the first quarter of the meeting. For a twenty-minute meeting, make sure it is stated in the first five minutes.
6. Follow the pace of the staffer. If it sounds like the staff is rushed or on a time crunch, forgo excessive pleasantries at the start and get right to the point.
7. Respect the policy of the office and avoid taking photographs in the meeting if the staffer says it is not permitted.

8. When you say you will get material to follow up, do so. Otherwise, you are not at the top of the list of possible technical advisors for the staff in the future. Trust me, you want to be on this list because the staff member would then be reaching out to you for advice when she or he needs it.

9. It is always appreciated when you send a follow-up "thank you" and "here are the documents we discussed" type of email within twenty-four hours after the meeting. Do not expect a reply.

6
How to Speak with Policymakers about Science

I f you do not remember anything else from this book, remember this: know your audience and have a strategy. Similar to the rest of this book, the following material is based on my personal experience. I imagine information here can be extrapolated to meet the needs of your country's political offices, as long as it is a democracy.

In general, when you speak with elected officials, you need to know who they are, where they came from, why they have the elite position they do, what their priorities are, and more. You need to do your homework. From there, you can strategize your delivery to your audience so that your message is impactful.

One of the most recent politically charged scientific topics is climate change. For years, I was one of the millions marching in the streets to support science. *Believe in science. Trust in science.* It wasn't until I worked on Capitol Hill and heard thoughts from all sides of the political spectrum that I understood why some people do not publicly support climate change–focused policy. Read this chapter to learn more about thoughts of politicians behind closed doors.

Here are the principles needed to strengthen your message:

Know your audience

As you have already seen with other examples throughout this book, the only way to change minds is to first understand the minds you are attempting to change. Elected officials are certainly a unique brand of people. From what I've observed from being on the front lines in Washington, DC, every elected official wants to make an impact for their cause, whatever that cause may be.

Regardless of one's own political viewpoint, we must respect the position a lawmaker has acquired. Remember, even if you do not respect the individual in that esteemed position, remind yourself that you respect *the position* itself. You respect the *office* and the people it represents. Another thing to remind yourself is that this political figure had to convince others to put them in their powerful role. It takes determination and insight to achieve such success.

You can learn a lot by simply observing the politician. A key tip while speaking to this group of people and their staff is— and remember this—if you do not show respect, your message will not be heard nor remembered, but you, unfortunately, will be remembered.

Lastly, before approaching a politician's office, ask yourself who is the elected official serving? Who do they answer to? Some powerful officials only answer to themselves (typically those at the end of their political careers or who may be considered megalomaniacs). If that is the case, then you need to do more sleuthing to determine the best mode of action and cultivate a conversation with an underlying message of appreciation for their past endeavors and achievements. On the other end of the spectrum, there are other officials who are only working in their voters' best interest—as determined by them, of course.

Have a strategy

Within a period of twelve months, I witnessed firsthand how politicians responded to international climate marches, national elections, a presidential impeachment, Black Lives Matter marches, lockdowns, economic collapse, quarantines, and COVID-19. Additionally, I worked on Capitol Hill at a time of intensely divisive politics. Even if a bill would benefit everybody regardless of who they are or where they are from, some politicians would not show support because they simply did not like the creator of the bill or thought supporting it may hurt their chances of being reelected.

An even more common occurrence in politics on Capitol Hill is when a politician is being asked to be the first person in their political party to support a bill, created by the "other" party. This can get dicey for the politician contemplating if publicly showing agreement with another party is a good strategy or not.

As a visiting scientist with a science-focused message and an agenda, and needing to gain support from less science-friendly politicians, I found the best technique to use in this situation is to speak with legislators who (1) are up for reelection soon and (2) come from a purple state (in other words, a swing state where Republicans and Democrats receive almost equal support). These politicians want to give the appearance that they are open-minded enough to support "the other team" (and gain more votes). Choose your audience wisely to save time and energy.

Convey your "elevator pitch" in the first minute

Present your policy in the same phrase as when you introduce yourself. "Thank you for meeting with me. I understand you are short on time and appreciate your interest in this [science] policy area. It is a pleasure to meet you, Senator, my name is [your name] and I am a [scientist]. I would like to discuss [XYZ] with you today."

Then explain why the policy needs to be supported or rejected with all the other techniques that you have learned in this book.

Know the politician's background

When trying to get more cosponsors (or elected officials) to publicly support my boss's science-based legislation, I gained substantial insight into the backgrounds of other Senators by conducting online searches and speaking with their staff. After identifying a legislator with a science background (or who has a scientist as a spouse or close relative), imagine how you would throw the policy pitch to them. What will you emphasize in the bill idea? What will you skip (if anything)?

General searches and active listening will take you far. Sometimes what is not said is more important than what is said. Keep your eyes and ears open.

Know the news. Be the news

Elected officials and Hill staffers are glued to the news. In addition to my typical obligations during the day on Capitol Hill, I read news articles at least twice daily of current events that pertained to my topics of interest and those of others. The articles either mentioned my boss, or the state, or a foreign affair that she was interested in.

It may surprise you to learn that elected officials have alerts set to determine when and where their name appears in publications. Therefore, if you like (or hate) a bill that your elected official has introduced and you write an opinion piece, be sure to mention the official's name and the piece of legislation you are referring to.

If you are writing an editorial for a newspaper or are being interviewed about something in your field that does not have a specific bill, law, or policy in place, consider saying something like this: "[X] cause is important because of [Y]. Senator [Z] should do [XYZ] about it." That will get the attention of their office and possibly even them, but only if the message and avenue of delivery, such as a major newspaper or television show, is impactful enough.

Know their priorities

This is different from knowing their background because interests could be personal interests, whereas, priorities are really what the politician wants to accomplish while in office. Their priorities significantly influence their political agenda (in other words, their career). An elected official's priorities and accomplishments are constantly referenced when they are up for reelection. In the House of Representatives, this is every two years. That is not long, particularly when you think about how difficult it is to create laws due to all of the negotiations that are involved.

If science or your specific area of expertise falls into the politician's priorities, you will see it mentioned in one way or another in their press releases. Don't know where to find those? Simply visit the website affiliated with the politician. Besides the press release section, these websites often have a "what so-and-so has done for the great state of x" section.

Scour through those sections and you will find what you are looking for.

If you want to search by legislative topics to find the most supportive elected officials in your area of interest, visit Congress. gov and type in the keyword in the search bar. You can then see who created bills on that topic and who supported those bills (in the cosponsors area of each bill). Beware, however, because you could be on that website for hours, a proverbial rabbit hole.

Know their voting histories

Voting history is sometimes the only thing that a politician can rely on to become reelected as referenced in the previous section. Politicians can have one opinion behind closed doors and then step outside into the gilded hallways of Congress and voice the exact opposite message to news reporters. Of one thing you can be certain: what they tell reporters is typically how they vote. Politicians do this to appease their voters, not necessarily because it is what they personally believe.

Is that good? Is that bad? You can decide that on your own, but if you want to get a politician on your side and promote science, be sure to review how they have previously voted on bills in your area of expertise. They are likely to repeat themselves unless there is a convincing argument otherwise. You can play to their personal interests (as noted before) or you play to their professional or public interests.

If they vote in the opposite way than what you would want, try to understand the reason why. Remember, everybody has a reason why they do something. Once you understand that, you can get creative with your messaging.

For the avid lobbyist in you: hobbies, family, and more

When speaking about One Health with a staff member of another senator's office, I learned that her boss once owned a turkey farm as a side business. In other words, the Senator was once a hobby farmer. From that experience, he already knew about bird flu and other zoonotic diseases (or diseases that can spread between animals and people). Therefore, the politician truly appreciated the economic consequences of a zoonotic disease on a community, industry, and a country. This Senator also knew how incredibly difficult it was to manage the bird flu virus.

It was helpful to understand this Senator's previous side business because he would be a likely supporter for future public health and zoonotic disease-focused legislation. When looking for bipartisan support, it is important to think of the person as a whole and not only as an elected official. Politicians have histories. Politicians have experiences. Politicians have hobbies. Use this background information to your advantage and tie it into your scientific message.

It may be beneficial to know the professions and interests of the politician's loved ones. The end goal here is that you want to become relatable to them early in the conversation. For instance, my boss's father was a physician and, therefore, she had immense respect for physicians. She understood the number of hours dedicated to training and what exactly is devoted to a career in medicine.

If it is not somebody's father, then maybe it is somebody else's wife who is the physician. Either way, if you want to advance a bill that is dedicated to health policy, describe a story showcasing how physicians can benefit.

The same principle applies to an agricultural policy if you learned that the politician's son-in-law is a farmer. Speak about how this science-based policy will help farmers increase their profit, crop supply, future business, and more.

How to approach controversial topics

Here, I will provide you with a strategy and a true story. It is important to actively listen to what an official's office says and doesn't say.

I was once speaking with a staff member from a conservative Republican Senator's office and had an epiphany. We were discussing One Health and happened upon the topic of climate change (and, of course, when I write "happened upon," I led the conversation there but did it in a nebulous way). I learned that the staffer believed in the science and that his boss recognized that the world is changing. However, there were two big problems that needed to be overcome if that Senator was to support any legislation that concerned climate change:

First, because of all the in-your-face climate-focused marches on Washington (imagine banging pots and pans outside of your office's front door and dozens of people trying to clamber into a space that was designed to comfortably fit a party of ten), climate change was no longer seen to be a scientific term; instead, it had become a politically charged liberal-agenda talking piece that could not and should not be supported by anybody in the Republican party. I was once candidly told by a conservative office that we had to remove the words *climate change* from our One Health bill or else we would not get any Republican support. We changed the words to *changes to the environment* and, soon after, gained two Republican supporters.

The **take-home message** here is that the words *climate change* are incredibly politically charged. That being said, you can still speak about climate change but avoid saying those two words in a row, at least during early relationship-building conversations with a conservative office—at least, for the immediate future.

And second, the other problem is that this particular Senator did not think climate change was related to humans' actions. Please refer to methods about how to manage this concern in chapter 4. Remember that a solid relationship needs to be built on mutual trust and respect before diving into the Carbon-13 and Carbon-14 topic. Also be sure to have reasonable (this means inexpensive) solutions ready to share. Nobody wants to hear of only problems, especially when there are no ideas for solutions. Use your scientific knowledge to provide at least three reasonable solutions and have them ready to deliver in case the politician asks for them.

Convince them to say "that's right"

One of the best ways to change a person's mind is to get into their mind first. I do not mean for you to manipulate them. Instead, I mean empathize with that person. See the world from their perspective. Listen to them before you speak. Listen to what they say *and* what they don't say. After that, tailor your message to meet *their* needs. Try to steer the conversation in a way to have them say "that's right" or "I agree" at least once. From that point on in a conversation, you will likely have a more intimate connection with the other person.

Advice for the doctors

If you have the word *doctor* associated with your name (like MD, DO, DVM, VMD, DDS, PhD, and any other "Dr." designation), it is important to realize that you have built-in respect with this title, even with politicians. There is no reason to flaunt the title, but rest assured that you are seen as an expert in your field and that your words typically carry more weight than others. Please remember, it is your responsibility to convey your scientific message in an appealing way that avoids jargon (unless indicated by the audience).

Most importantly: know their staff

This topic brings us full circle. If you are liked by the office staff (particularly Legislative Assistants) and you have successfully convinced them to support your mission, then you likely have increased the chance of having the politician publicly support the measure. The **take-home message** here is this: if you don't personally know the politician, then you should commit your time and energy to win favor with the staffers. After all, these people are constantly around their boss while providing them advice in their specialty area(s). Trust me, you want the staffers to be on your side. That way, you have a better chance of (indirectly) motivating the politician to support science-friendly legislation.

7

Life from the Other Side
of the Boardroom Table

S o far, you have heard that it is important to visualize the conversation from your target audience's perspective. With this chapter and its corresponding material in the appendix, I wanted to show you what life really is like for congressional staff (particularly Legislative Assistants) and for you to see how bills and policy get made. In this chapter, I will show you how law text (or "legislation") can be translated into attractive everyday speech. Now that you know how to translate science into laymen's terms, it is time to look across the boardroom table and pretend to live the life of a Senate staffer. *After all, how else can you effectively communicate with your target audience if you can't imagine being in their position?*

This chapter is meant for you to challenge yourself. Yes, I did save the best for last. See how much you have learned and grown with your new knowledge with an activity.

Here are the rules: After reading a feasible One Health bill (Appendix A), create a one-page memo about the bill for your Senator boss. In this memo, you will be asking for permission to reach scientific experts outside of Congress to review the bill and provide feedback (this is called "technical assistance").

For memo writing, here is a tip- the memo needs to have four sections that include:

1. New bill idea summary.
2. What problem the bill solves (This part answers several questions: What's the best reason *to* introduce this bill? What's the best reason *not to* introduce this bill? *Think about who the supporters and detractors are.* How would this bill impact the home state? Could the bill potentially cause a headache for your boss? Would this bill come back to haunt your boss if she or he decides to run for president in 20 years? If your boss is of the mindset that Presidency is in the future, this last question may be the most important of them all- what is the media hook?)
3. *How* this bill would address the problem.
4. Final recommendation for your boss.

After you are done with writing your staff memo asking for technical assistance from your Senator boss, your next assignment is to draft a one-pager to convince staff in other Senate offices to bring the One Health bill to their own boss to publicly support (cosponsor). Remember, the other staffers will need to (1) feel compelled to create a memo for their boss and (2) convince their boss that the bill is worth supporting. Every boss is different so good luck!

After you have completed *both* activities, look at Appendix B and C and examine the differences between your version and mine.

In the Appendices, you will find:

1. A sample One Health bill.
    a. This sample bill pertains to a large network of scientists, engineers, public health professionals, and people of

other disciplines. All readers would have a stake in this legislation if it were to pass into law.

2. A corresponding sample staff memo that a Senate staffer (who likely created the bill) would write for her or his boss. This memo asks permission to seek scientific technical assistance outside of the confidential Congressional Research Service. (This means that the staffer may be contacting *you* for your input on the science-based bill.)

3. A cosponsor one-pager.

Epilogue

At this point, you have been given a lot of information. Feel free to put the book down, digest the information over the next week, then revisit the book and test yourself- how much of it do you remember? Ultimately, these techniques will serve you well in your future communication endeavors but it works best with practice. As mentioned in the chapter entitled How to Speak with the Public about Science, I cannot overemphasize the importance of joining a weekly or biweekly public speaking group (like Toastmasters), particularly with large clubs of over twenty people who are highly experienced. Your mission is to find the group where you can learn the most- settle into a group where you are the weakest speaker of them all- that way, you have more room to grow. I am aware that there are other public speaking options available but I do not have personal experience with them. All I can tell you is what I know and what I have experienced.

In preparation for communicating a new idea to another person, do as much background reading as possible about your target audience. It will help the conversation flow and, as mentioned in the chapters about communicating with policymakers and their staff, brevity is key. As a science policy advisor working in the United States Senate, I quickly learned that having "more white on the page than ink" is the best rule to follow. It is a challenge, particularly at the start, but like anything else, practice makes perfect. Happy practicing!

Appendix A:
Sample One Health Bill

Title: To permanently establish the successful interagency collaborative system that developed during the COVID-19 pandemic and for other purposes.

Be it enacted by the Senate and House of Representatives of the United States of America in Congress assembled,

SECTION 1. SHORT TITLE.

This Act may be cited as the "Sustainability through One Health Act of 2021."

SEC. 2. FINDINGS.

Congress makes the following findings:

(1) A disease outbreak anywhere is a global concern.

(2) During the COVID-19 pandemic, the One Health Office of the National Center for Emerging and Zoonotic Infectious Diseases of the Centers for Disease Control and Prevention created a temporary One Health Federal Interagency COVID-19 Coordination Group comprised of career scientists of various disciplines to take action to prevent future pandemics.

(3) The One Health approach brings human, animal, environmental, and ecosystem health expertise together to prevent, respond to, and mitigate disease outbreaks.

(4) New, reemerging, and zoonotic infections have high societal and economic costs. The enormous costs of pandemics can be averted with proactive strategic investments in capacity building and preparedness through the One Health approach.

(5) Zoonotic diseases are more likely to spread from animals to people when there is unnatural close proximity between animals and people, including at live animal markets, and where there is loss of biodiversity and natural habitat.

(6) When an animal species goes extinct or a wild animal's natural habitat is degraded, the ecosystem's food chain is altered, causing unsustainable competition and stress in the remaining animals that subsequently move closer to people to seek food and shelter. This unnatural close proximity between animals and people increases the risk of a spillover event.

(7) Zoonotic diseases are responsible for—

    (A) approximately 60 percent of all human infections;

    (B) up to 75 percent of new or emerging infectious diseases affecting humans; and

    (C) more than 80 percent of biological agents that could be intentionally released as biological weapons.

SEC. 3. ESTABLISHMENT OF THE STANDING INTERAGENCY ONE HEALTH COMMITTEE.

(a) Establishment.—There is established within the Centers for Disease Control and Prevention the Standing Interagency One Health Committee (in this Act referred to as the "Committee").

(b) Membership.—

    (1) Composition.—The Committee shall be composed of a Chair as described in paragraph (2) and the additional members described in paragraph (3).

    (2) Committee chair.—

        (A) Appointment.— The Secretary of Health and Human Services shall appoint the Chair, in accordance with subparagraph (B), who shall be an officer of the United States.

        (B) Qualifications.—The Chair—

            (i) shall have—

                (I) experience orchestrating complex whole-of-government operations; and

                (II) experience in global health emergencies, including experience in animal health and environmental health; and

            (ii) may be the Director of the One Health Office of the National Center for Emerging and Zoonotic Infectious Diseases of the Centers for Disease Control and Prevention.

        (C) Term.—The Chair shall serve for a term of 6 years and may be reappointed for subsequent terms.

    (3) Additional members.—In addition to the Chair, the Committee shall include—

        (A) the head (or the designee of such head) of—

            (i) the Department of Health and Human Services;

            (ii) the Centers for Disease Control and Prevention;

            (iii) the National Institutes of Health;

            (iv) the National Institute of Allergy and Infectious Diseases of the National Institutes of Health;

            (v) the Food and Drug Administration;

            (vi) the Center for Veterinary Medicine of the Food and Drug Administration;

            (vii) the Center for Food Safety and Applied Nutrition of the Food and Drug Administration;

            (viii) the Department of Agriculture;

            (ix) the Animal and Plant Health Inspection Service of the Department of Agriculture;

            (x) the Plants Protection and Quarantine program of the Animal and Plant Health Inspection Service of the Department of Agriculture;

            (xi) Veterinary Services of the Animal and Plant Health Inspection Service of the Department of Agriculture;

            (xii) the National Animal Health Laboratory Network of Veterinary

	Services of the Animal and Plant Health Inspection Service of the Department of Agriculture;
(xiii)	Wildlife Services of the Animal and Plant Health Inspection Service of the Department of Agriculture;
(xiv)	the Agricultural Research Service of the Department of Agriculture;
(xv)	the Food Safety and Inspection Service of the Department of Agriculture;
(xvi)	the Environmental Protection Agency;
(xvii)	the Office of Water of the Environmental Protection Agency;
(xviii)	the Office of Air Quality Planning and Standards of the Environmental Protection Agency;
(xix)	the Department of the Interior;
(xx)	the United States Fish and Wildlife Service of the Department of the Interior;
(xxi)	the United States Geological Survey of the Department of the Interior;
(xxii)	the National Wildlife Health Center of the United States Geological Survey of the Department of the Interior;
(xxiii)	the National Park Service of the Department of the Interior;
(xxiv)	the Department of State;
(xxv)	the United States Agency for International Development of the Department of State;
(xxvi)	the Bureau of International Narcotics and Law Enforcement Affairs of the Department of State;
(xxvii)	the Department of Defense;
(xxviii)	the Defense Health Agency of the Department of Defense;
(xxix)	the Defense Threat Reduction Agency of the Department of Defense;
(xxx)	the Department of Homeland Security;
(xxxi)	U.S. Immigration and Customs Enforcement;
(xxxii)	the Science and Technology Directorate of the Department of Homeland Security;
(xxxiii)	the National Intelligence Council of the Office of the Director of National Intelligence;
(xxxiv)	the Department of Justice;
(xxxv)	the Environment and Natural Resources Division of the Department of Justice;
(xxxvi)	the Department of Commerce;
(xxxvii)	the National Oceanic and Atmospheric Administration;
(xxxviii)	the National Aeronautics and Space Administration;
(xxxix)	the Office of Science and Technology Policy;
(xl)	the National Science Foundation;
(xli)	the Department of Education; and
(xlii)	any other relevant Federal agency determined by the Chair;

    (B) a representative from the intelligence community (as defined in section 3 of the National Security Act of 1947 (50 U.S.C. 3003)), as determined by the Chair; and

    (C) any other representative determined relevant by the Chair, including from academic institutions or other individuals from the private sector.

  (4) Nonvoting members.—Any member of the Committee described in paragraph (3)(C) who is not an officer or employee of the Federal Government shall serve as a nonvoting member of the Committee.

(c) Duties of the Committee.—

  (1) In general.—

    (A) Duties of the committee.—The Committee shall meet not less frequently than once every quarter to—

      (i) establish and coordinate interagency efforts with respect to the objectives described in paragraph (2), including through memoranda of understanding between the Federal agencies or interagency agreements to carry out projects with respect to such objectives;

      (ii) recommend to the Chair how the appropriations under subsection (g) shall be allocated to support the interagency efforts described in subparagraph (A); and

      (iii) prepare the reports described in paragraph (4)(A).

    (B) Duty of the chair.—After considering the recommendations of the Committee under subparagraph (A)(ii), the Chair shall determine how the appropriations under subsection (g) shall be allocated to support the interagency efforts described in subparagraph (A)(i).

  (2) Objectives.—The objectives described in this paragraph are each of the following:

    (A) Promoting comprehensive surveillance, reporting, and preventive measures and real-time monitoring programs focused on infectious and zoonotic diseases, domestically and internationally in—

      (i) people;

      (ii) companion animals;

      (iii wildlife and zoo animals;

      (iv) livestock; and

      (v) other domesticated animals.

    (B) Promoting wildlife management and conservation through—

      (i) protection of natural habitats;

      (ii) biodiversity protection; and

      (iii) increased law enforcement to combat wildlife trafficking.

    (C) Ensuring food safety and food security in areas that have previously been dependent on wildlife meat as a dietary protein source and creating capacity building programs for ensuring food safety and food security in such areas.

    (D) Expanding research and development of a coordinated and comprehensive nationwide laboratory data sharing system to address—

      (i) health concerns related to diseases and other health conditions in—

        (I)   people;

        (II)   wildlife and zoo animals;

        (III) companion animals;

        (IV) livestock; and

        (V)   other domesticated animals used for their products; or

(ii) any other concerns that are related to—

        (I)   zoonotic diseases;

        (II)   environmental hazards and risk factors affecting public health; and

        (III) antimicrobial resistance.

(E) Expanding domestic and international health literacy, communication, and education programs for children and adults that are aimed to prevent and mitigate spillover events and their consequences, including a pandemic.

(F) Establishing and implementing a strategy to improve domestic public health and veterinary public health national infrastructures in a manner that—

    (i) through the prevention of disease, results in the Federal Government spending 25 percent less on health care by the date that is 10 years after the date of enactment of this Act than the Federal Government spends on health care as of such date of enactment; and

    (ii) streamlines interagency efforts resulting in improved health and well-being of people and animals.

(G) Increasing law enforcement efforts related to combating illegal animal fighting.

(3) Voting.—All decisions of the Committee with respect to the activities under paragraph (1) shall be made by majority vote of the members present and voting.

(4) Reporting.—

(A) In general.—The Committee shall prepare biannual reports on the activities described in subparagraphs (A) and (B) of paragraph (1), including outcomes from such activities. Each such report shall be—

    (i) submitted to—

        (I)   the Committee on Health, Education, Labor, and Pensions of the Senate;

        (II)   the Committee on Agriculture, Nutrition, and Forestry of the Senate;

        (III) the Committee on Foreign Relations of the Senate;

        (IV) the Committee on Armed Services of the Senate;

        (V)   the Committee on Appropriations of the Senate;

        (VI) the Committee on Energy and Commerce of the House of Representatives;

        (VII) the Committee on Agriculture of the House of Representatives;

        (VIII) the Committee on Natural Resources of the House of

Representatives;

    (IX) the Committee on Foreign Affairs of the House of Representatives;

    (X) the Committee on Armed Services of the House of Representatives; and

    (XI) the Committee on Appropriations of the House of Representatives; and

  (ii) publicly posted on the website of the One Health Office of the National Center for Emerging and Zoonotic Infectious Diseases of the Centers for Disease Control and Prevention.

  (B) Reporting during public health emergencies.—During a public health emergency (as defined in section 319 of the Public Health Service Act (42 U.S.C. 247d)), the Chair shall—

    (i) be the principal advisor to the President and the Secretary of Health and Human Services on the activities described in subparagraphs (A) and (B) of paragraph (1); and

    (ii) report to the President and the Secretary of Health and Human Services, without being required to report through any other official of the Administration or the Department of Health and Human Services.

(d) Noncompensation.—The Chair and additional members of the Committee shall serve on the Committee without additional pay for such membership.

(e) Supplement Not Supplant.—Any funds made available for a project under this Act shall supplement and not supplant any other Federal, State, or local funds expended for such project.

(f) Definitions.—In this Act:

  (1) One health approach.—The term "One Health approach" means a collaborative, multisectoral, and transdisciplinary approach, working at the local, regional, national, and global levels, with the goal of achieving optimal health outcomes while recognizing the interconnection between people, animals, plants, and their shared environments.

  (2) Spillover event.—The term "spillover event" means an event during which a pathogen from one species moves into another species.

  (3) Zoonotic disease.—The term "zoonotic disease" means an illness caused by a—

    (A) virus;

    (B) bacteria;

    (C) parasite;

    (D) fungus;

    (E) prion; or

    (F) other microbe that spreads between animals and people.

(g) Authorization of Appropriations.—There is authorized to be appropriated for fiscal year 2022 and each fiscal year thereafter, $500,000,000, to remain available until expended, to the Chair for carrying out the duties under subsection (c)(1)(B).

Appendix B:
Sample Staff Memo to Seek Technical Assistance

MEMO

TO: Senator ZZZ
FROM: [Your name and names of colleagues]
DATE: [Month, Day, Year]
SUBJECT: NEW BILL IDEA: Codify ad hoc interagency COVID-19 committee

NEW BILL IDEA: In response to the pandemic, the CDC created an ad hoc interagency working group to respond to, mitigate, and prevent pandemics. Once the current pandemic has ended, the ad hoc group is expected to disband. *Staff recommend introducing a bill to permanently establish and fund this interagency group so the country is better protected against future pandemics.*

What the problem is:
- Prior to the Trump Administration, federal pandemic preparation efforts were coordinated by a single ad hoc team on the National Security Council. Since this team was disbanded in 2018, several scientists working in the CDC were forced to create their own ad hoc interagency working group. This group has been successful in mitigating disease exposure between animals and people (like seen in the Bronx Zoo with the tigers and lions). However, the group's influence is limited because not all agencies recognize the importance of effective interagency communication to stop disease spread.

How this bill would address it:
- Establish in statute an interagency committee comprised of career staff of relevant federal agencies to coordinate longer-term federal policies and support efforts to help prevent future pandemics, including:
  - Improve disease surveillance and management systems (in both people and animals where the diseases come from). This can help address [name disease] in [your state].
  - Promote natural habitat conservation and other environmentally friendly actions for agriculture and wildlife [some industry may have concern(s) here].
  - Mitigate antibiotic resistance.
  - Increase law enforcement in wildlife trafficking and animal fighting [financial investment to decrease risk of disease transfer between countries].

Recommendation: <u>Authorize staff to seek technical assistance.</u> It is clear now that pandemic preparedness coordination must be a permanent federal effort established in law that really digs into the underlying issues, and not something ad hoc that can just be created and disbanded at any time.

Agree with staff recommendation?   Agree _____   Disagree _____

Appendix C:
Sample One-Pager
Sustainability through One Health Act of 2021

Senator XXXXXX invites your boss to cosponsor this crucial bill to prevent future pandemics.

Current Situation: In response to the COVID pandemic, the CDC created an ad hoc interagency working group (called the *"One Health Federal Interagency COVID-19 Coordination Group"*) to respond to, mitigate, and prevent pandemics. Once the current pandemic is done, this ad hoc group is expected to disband. *The "Sustainability through One Health Act" permanently establishes and funds this interagency group so the country is better protected against future pandemics.*

More information about the "One Health Federal Interagency COVID-19 Coordination Group":
- Created in February 2020 in response to COVID-19 by career scientists.
- It is a coordination platform across agencies that allows for collaboration and rapid information-sharing across sectors while also facilitating alignment of research, priorities, and messaging regarding the human, animal, and environmental aspects of COVID-19.

Underlying problems of pandemics:
- When an animal species goes extinct or a wild animal's natural habitat is degraded, the ecosystem's food chain is altered, causing unsustainable competition and stress in the remaining animals that subsequently move closer to people to seek food and shelter. Any unnatural close proximity between wildlife, livestock, companion animals and people (either in a live animal market or near a degrading habitat) increases the risk of disease spread between animals and people.

How this bill would address the underlying problems of pandemics:
- Establish in statute an interagency committee comprised of career staff of relevant federal agencies to coordinate long-term federal policies and support efforts to help prevent future pandemics, including:
  - Improve disease surveillance and public health infrastructure
  - Promote natural habitat conservation and other environmentally friendly actions for agriculture and wildlife
  - Mitigate antibiotic resistance across species
  - Increase law enforcement in wildlife trafficking and animal fighting
  - Implement strategies to promote food safety and security in communities that depend on wildlife for dietary protein source.

Authorization of Appropriations: $500 million annually to the interagency committee as supplemental funds to achieve the goals set forth in the bill to mitigate and prevent any future pandemics. The Committee members vote to create formal recommendations to The Committee Chair (who is appointed by the Secretary of HHS) and the Chair distributes the supplemental funding to the interagency programs.

Contact: XXX_YYY@ZZZZZ.senate.gov

Acknowledgments

This book is the result of lessons learned and experiences gained over many years, thanks to the support of my family and friends. Mom and Dad, I am who I am because you raised me and you continue to lift me up, even when I fall. I am forever grateful. Jason, Jeff, and Janet, thank you for your love and support. I am inspired by you every day.

To my scientist, engineering, veterinary, and other professional science friends who have provided honest feedback throughout this book development process, I am grateful for your support and fine attention to detail.

Thank you, Betty Wan, Raheel Mahmood, MS, Vanessa Nichols, S.B. Meridian, Karla López, and Kyle Novak, PhD, for being willing to be the reviewers of the first draft. I hope you can spot a few changes made since that time.

To my teacher friends, Tyler Chuck, Jonté Lee, and Robin Schader, PhD, thank you for providing great feedback on the chapter about working with children. Your students are lucky to have you in their lives.

To my science communication friends, Andrea Stathopoulos, PhD, Sanae ElShourbagy Ferreira, PhD, Jerome Seid, MD, and Amy Bond, MS, thank you for providing your thoughts on the chapter about communicating with people outside a scientist's immediate field.

To my policy friends on and off the Hill—Tristan Brown, JD, John Watts, JD, Lt. JJ Johnson, Jacob Pasner, PhD, Matt Holland, DVM, Melissa Melton, MPH, Shadi Mamaghani,

PhD, Kate Wall, JD, Adrian Hochstadt, JD, CAE, and Heather Case, DVM, MPH, DACVPM, CAE, thank you for reading (and sometimes rereading) the book. I would be remiss to not thank those who helped my policy knowledge grow exponentially throughout my time on the Hill; therefore, special thanks go to: Josh, Andrew, Joe P., Joe V., Justin, Lizzy, Serena, Rishi, Alec, Eric, Laurel, Deanna, Alexandra, Haley, Rachel, Tom, and David. Your insights have strengthened the book's message, and I'm certain the policy advice is sound and will help many.

Thank you, Salvador Saenz, for your talented cover illustration.

Outside of the book but for those who have contributed to my professional growth, I wanted to express my appreciation to some well-deserving groups. Thank you to Community Resources for Science (a fabulous non-profit organization in California) for supporting One Health education. Thank you, American Veterinary Medical Association, for selecting me as the 2019–2020 Science and Engineering Policy Fellow. In addition, gratitude goes to the American Association for the Advancement of Science for training me in preparation for my time on the Hill.

Last and certainly not least, I thank my personal and professional role model, Senator Dianne Feinstein, who is a brilliant policymaker with great integrity and a nonstop work ethic. It was a dream come true to serve you and the great state of California. You have taught me more than I could have ever imagined. Thank you for your leadership.

About the Author

Photo Credit: Mark Serr

DR. DEBORAH THOMSON is a veterinarian and One Health advocate who started teaching in 2001. Since then, she has served as a Science Policy Advisor in the United States Senate; has founded and led a global organization that inspires children and adults to value the interconnection between human health and the health of the environment, plants, and animals (called One Health Lessons); has practiced clinical veterinary medicine in emergency departments, animal shelters, and general practices; has taught thousands of children about One Health; has worked as a One Health Expert Consultant in multiple global nongovernmental organizations including the World Veterinary Association's One Health Education Subgroup Committee and EcoHealth Alliance; has also consulted for the One Health Institute at the University of California–Davis; has served as an external member of the United Nations' Food and Agriculture Organization's One Health Work Group; has created internationally acclaimed science lessons that are being translated into over eighty languages; and has been running a Science

Communication Training program with over 800 global participants.

In addition, she has won multiple public speaking competitions, has spoken in over a dozen countries, and has most notably been an invited speaker at events associated with the US Centers for Disease Control and Prevention, the Global Health Security Agenda, the US Agency for International Development, the US Department of Agriculture, National Aeronautics and Space Administration (NASA), the World Veterinary Association, and the One Health Action Collaborative, an ad hoc activity associated with the Forum on Microbial Threats at the National Academies of Sciences, Engineering, and Medicine.

Dr. Thomson has been recognized as a Global Goodwill Ambassador, a distinction reserved for humanitarians, as well as an Impact Leader and an Excellence in STEM Inspiration Honoree. Her articles have been printed in multiple publications, including *The Lancet Planetary Health*.

Aside from writing and working on these worthy projects, she enjoys playing music, traveling, learning languages, and being outdoors. She lives in the Washington, DC area.